ENGLISH
FRENCH

Bilingual lessons and reproducible activities teaching beginners.

by
Marie-France Marcie
and
Barbara Rankie

ISBN: 978-1-55386-122-5

Acknowledgements
Remerciements

Authors – Marie-France Marcie, Barbara Rankie

Cover Design – Campbell Creative Services

Editors – Andrew Gaiero, Sara Jordan, Peter Lebuis

Illustrations – Various Contributors

Interior Layout – Darryl Taylor, Andrew Gaiero

We suggest the purchase of our companion CD/book kit, *Bilingual Beginners: English-French*, which uses curriculum-based songs to enhance and complement the material presented in this book.

Nous vous suggérons d'acheter l'ensemble d'accompagnement CD/livre, Bilingual Beginners: English-French, *qui utilise de la musique pour enseigner le matériel présenté dans ce livre.*

For further information contact:

Jordan Music Productions Inc.
M.P.O. Box 490
Niagara Falls, NY
U.S.A. 14302-0490

Jordan Music Productions Inc.
Station M, Box 160
Toronto, Ontario
Canada, M6S 4T3

Telephone: 1-800-567-7733
Web Site: www.SongsThatTeach.com
E-mail: sjordan@sara-jordan.com

We acknowledge the financial support of the Government of Canada through the Book Publishing Industry Development Program (BPIDP) for our publishing activities.

Canada

List of Skills Covered in This Book
Liste des habiletés couvertes dans ce livre

Oral Communication / *Communication orale*

– the ability to follow French/English instructions and suggestions
– visual and verbal skills using repetition
– the promotion of cultural exchange with native French/English speakers
– the development of critical thinking skills

Writing / *Écriture*

– the ability to follow articulated sequences of instruction where each topic builds upon those of preceding levels
– written exercises helping students gain an appreciation of French/English cultures

Reading / *Lecture*

– reading simple material
– reading and responding to comprehension activities
– engaging in written material providing a complete learning experience:
  - answering short questions
  - word boxes
  - filling in missing words
  - finding secret messages
  - coloring activities
  - matching columns
  - drawing pictures
  - signs
  - song lyrics (if used with the the corresponding *Bilingual Beginners: English–French* CD/Book kit)

Grammar / *Grammaire*

– interrogative, affirmative and negative constructions
– nouns and pronouns
– gender of nouns in French
– prepositions
– definite article *the* and *le, la, les*
– present tense of the verb "to like" (*aimer*)

Vocabulary Building / *Vocabulaire*

– integration of new words into lessons and exercises
– using basic vocabulary such as: greetings, colors, numbers, animals, time expressions, food, family members, parts of the body, etc.
– vocabulary building exercises including crosswords

Spelling Words and Strategies / *Orthographie et stratégies*

– alphabetization

Standards of Foreign Language Learning
Normes d'apprentissage d'une langue étrangère

The concepts taught in this book comply with the five major organizing principles of the "Standards of Foreign Language Learning" in the following ways:

Communication in French

a) using conversation to provide and obtain information; expressing feelings and emotions, and exchanging opinions
b) understanding and interpreting spoken and written French
c) presenting information, concepts, and ideas in French

Cultures of the World

a) understanding Francophone cultural behaviors: gestures, oral expressions for greetings, cultural activities such as games, foods, etc.
b) developing an awareness of the products from Francophone cultures: food and children's songs

Connections to Other Disciplines

a) demonstrating, in French, an understanding of other subject areas such as the categorization of animals, and family members
b) reading, listening to, and talking about short stories, poems and songs in French

Comparisons and Insights into the Nature of Language and Culture

a) understanding similarities and differences between English and French
b) being aware of idiomatic expressions, formal and informal forms of the language

Communities at Home and Abroad

a) conveying messages to French speakers in person, email, letters, etc.
b) performing skits and songs in French for school and community celebrations
c) becoming life-long learners by using French for enrichment and enjoyment: stories, children's web pages, children's programs and latin music
d) establishing friendships within the local French-speaking community

Table of Contents
Table des matières

10. Opposites / Les contraires

11. Food and Family / La nourriture et la famille

12. Parts of the Body / Les parties du corps

Tips for Teachers and Parents

The *Bilingual Kids: English–French* series which can be used independently or as a companion resource supplementing the *Bilingual Songs: English–French* audio series. This book teaches greetings, the alphabet, vowels, consonants, counting to twelve, telling time, animals, colors, food and family members in both languages. Each lesson includes a teacher-directed group activity, as well as individual activities which may be reproduced for the class.

A suggested vocabulary list (with translations) is provided at the beginning of each chapter. Word cards needed for the teacher-directed activities can be printed from our website at: http://www.SongsThatTeach.com/BilingualFrenchWordCards

We are very pleased to have teachers Marie-France Marcie and Barbara Rankie co-author this series. Marie-France comes from La Loupe, France, near Paris. After studying at the University of Tours in France, she moved to Canada and attended Brock University. She earned her B.Ed. in France and a B.A. in Languages in Canada. An experienced French teacher with 28 years of experience, she is presently freelancing as a consultant, translating educational materials.

Barbara Rankie, with a B.A. in Linguistics and Psychology from the University of Ottawa and a B.Ed. from Queens University, has been a teacher with the District School Board of Niagara for the past 20 years. She is highly regarded by her colleagues for her creative lessons.

Please visit our website, www.SongsThatTeach.com, to further enhance classroom learning. You'll find pen pal classes from around the world, contests, cartooning lessons and much more.

Enjoy!

Sara Jordan
President

Suggested Vocabulary List
Liste de vocabulaire

À plus tard!	See you later!
belle journée	beautiful day
Bonne nuit	Good night
Bonjour	Good morning
Ça va bien	I'm well
Comment ça va?	How are you?
Content de te voir	Nice to meet you
De rien	You're welcome
Je m'appelle	My name is
Merci	Thank you
Salut	Hello!
nombres	numbers
un	one
deux	two
trois	three
quatre	four
cinq	five
six	six
sept	seven
huit	eight
neuf	nine
dix	ten
onze	eleven
douze	twelve

Group Lesson

Materials: number cards

Preparation: Make number cards or print them out from our website at: http://www.SongsThatTeach.com/BilingualFrenchWordCards

How it Works:
Have a student draw a number card. Ask one student to give the English word for the number and another student to give the French word. As a group, chant both words and have the class do an action the number of times shown on the card. Continue using numbers to twelve.

Activité de groupe

Matériel: cartes numérotées

Préparation: Faites des cartes numérotées ou bien imprimez-les sur le site web à: http://www.SongsThatTeach.com/BilingualFrenchWordCards

Comment faire:
Un élève tire une carte numérotée. Un autre élève donne l'anglais pour le nombre et un autre élève donne le français. Faites chanter les 2 mots par tous les élèves et demandez-leur de faire une action.

Activity 1 / Activité 1

Trace the letters and the numbers.

Trace les lettres et les nombres.

one   1  un

two 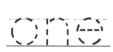 2 deux

three 3 trois

four 4 quatre

five 5 cinq

six 6 six

Bilingual Kids: English–French, Beginners © 2010 Sara Jordan Publishing

Activity 2 / Activité 2

Trace the letters and the numbers.

Trace les lettres et les nombres.

seven	7 	sept
eight 	8	huit
nine	9	neuf
ten	10	dix
eleven	11	onze
twelve 	12	douze

Activity 3 / Activité 3

Trace the letters.

Trace les lettres.

Hello.

Salut.

My name is _____.

Je m'appelle _____.

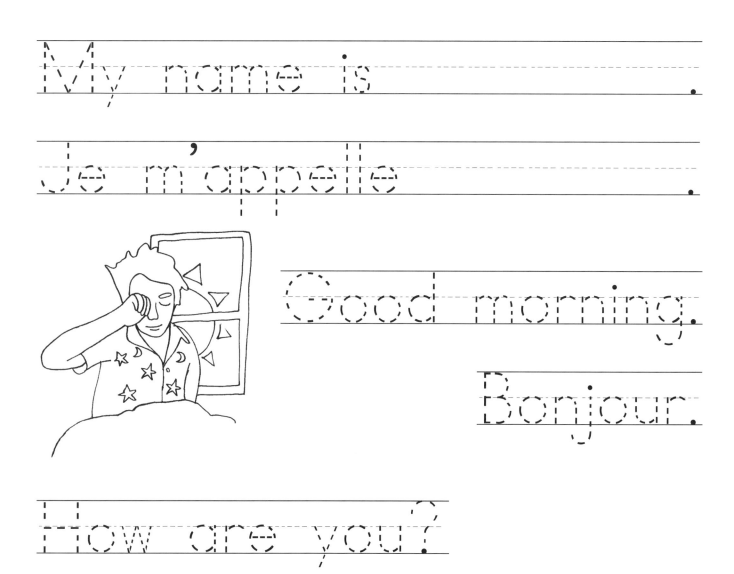

Good morning.

Bonjour.

How are you?

Comment ça va?

  Bilingual Kids: English-French, Beginners   © 2010 Sara Jordan Publishing

Activity 4 / Activité 4

Print the French expressions into the shape puzzles.

Écris les mots en français dans les cases.

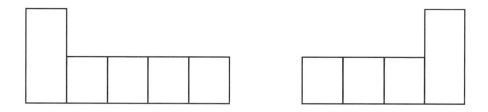

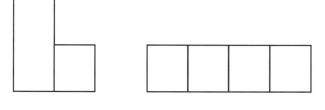

Word Bank / Liste de mots
- *au revoir*
- *bonne nuit*
- *ça va bien*
- *de rien*
- *merci*

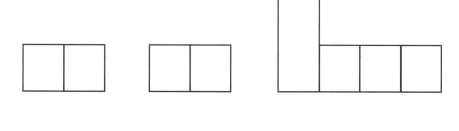

Activity 5 / Activité 5

Complete the story in your new language.

Complète l'histoire dans ta nouvelle langue.

Word Bank / Liste de mots

How are you? / *Comment ça va?*	I'm well. / *Ça va bien.*
See you later! / *À plus tard!*	Good-bye. / *Au revoir.*

Group Lesson

Materials: alphabet

How it Works:
Review the letters of the alphabet for both languages.
Then display the alphabet with several letters covered.
Have students identify the missing letters, in French and
English either through chanting or singing the alphabet.

Activité de groupe

Matériel: l'alphabet

Comment faire:
Révisez les lettres de l'alphabet dans les deux langues, puis
montrez l'alphabet avec des lettres cachées. Demandez aux
élèves d'identifier les lettres qui manquent en chantant.

Suggested Vocabulary List
Liste de vocabulaire

après	after
avant	before
(le) cheval	horse
(les) consonnes	consonants
entre	between
(le) garçon	boy
(les) lettres	letters
(l') oeuf	egg
(la) veste	jacket
(les) voyelles	vowels

Activity 1 / Activité 1

Trace the letters of the alphabet.

Trace les lettres de l'alphabet.

Aa Bb Cc Dd

Ee Ff Gg Hh

Ii Jj Kk Ll

Mm Nn Oo Pp

Qq Rr Ss Tt

Uu Vv Ww Xx

Yy Zz

Bilingual Kids: English-French, Beginners   © 2010 Sara Jordan Publishing

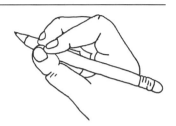

Activity 2 / Activité 2

Fill in the missing letters.

Complète avec les lettres qui manquent.

Which letter comes...

Quelle lettre vient...

after F?

après F?

D E F

before I?

avant I?

I J K

between O and Q?

entre O et Q?

O Q

Activity 3 / Activité 3

Fill in the missing letters.

Complète avec les lettres qui manquent.

Which letter comes...

Quelle lettre vient...

after V?

après V ?

before M?

avant M ?

in between N and P?

entre N et P ?

Bilingual Kids: English-French, Beginners   © 2010 Sara Jordan Publishing

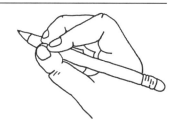

Activity 4 / Activité 4

List the numbers in your new language, from one through twelve, in alphabetical order.

Écris les nombres de un à douze dans ta nouvelle langue en ordre alphabétique.

Word Bank / Liste de mots					
one / *un*	two / *deux*	three / *trois*	four / *quatre*	five / *cinq*	six / *six*
seven / *sept*	eight / *huit*	nine / *neuf*	ten / *dix*	eleven / *onze*	twelve / *douze*

Activity 5 / Activité 5

Color the object that does not belong. Then look for the word in the word bank and print it at the side in your new language.

Colorie ce qui est différen puis trouve le mot dans la liste et écris-le à côté dans ta nouvelle langue.

Word Bank / Liste de mots

jacket / *la veste*   egg / *l'oeuf*   boy / *le garçon*   horse / *le cheval*

Bilingual Kids: English-French, Beginners © 2010 Sara Jordan Publishing

Suggested Vocabulary List
Liste de vocabulaire

(l') anniversaire	birthday
(le) ballon	balloon
bleu	blue
(la) bougie	candle
brun	brown
(le) gâteau	cake
jaune	yellow
noir	black
orange	orange
rose	pink
rouge	red
vert	green
violet	purple
J'aime	I like
Je n'aime pas	I don't like
Et toi ?	And you?
Et vous ?	And you? (formal/plural)

Group Lesson

Materials: construction paper of various colors (yellow, purple, red, blue, black, brown, orange, pink, green, white)

Preparation: Make balloons out of construction paper. Print the names of the colors in both languages on each balloon.

How it Works:

Review the color words in both languages first. Have students sit in a circle and explain to them that they will need to listen to the questions carefully so they will know when to stand. Start by holding a balloon and say, "I like black. Do you?" Students who like the color black stand and respond together by saying, "J'aime le noir." The children who do not like the color, remain seated and respond by saying, "Je n'aime pas le noir." Continue by interchanging English and French, i.e., "J'aime l'orange. Et vous?" Students respond in either English or French.

Activité de groupe

Matériel: papier de construction de différentes couleurs (jaune, violet, rouge, bleu, noir, brun, orange, rose, vert, blanc)

Préparation: Faites des ballons avec le papier de construction. Écrivez le nom des couleurs en français et en anglais dans chaque ballon.

Comment faire:

Révisez d'abord les couleurs en français et en anglais. Faites asseoir les élèves en rond et expliquez-leur qu'ils doivent écouter attentivement pour savoir quand ils doivent se lever. Prenez un ballon et dites : « J'aime le noir. Et vous ? » Les élèves qui aiment le noir se lèvent et disent : « J'aime le noir. » Les élèves qui n'aiment pas le noir se restent assis et disent : « Je n'aime pas le noir. » Continuez en interchangeant l'anglais et le français, ex : « I like orange. Do you? » Les élèves peuvent répondre en anglais ou en français.

Activity 1 / Activité 1

Color the palette and trace the words.

Colorie la palette et trace les mots.

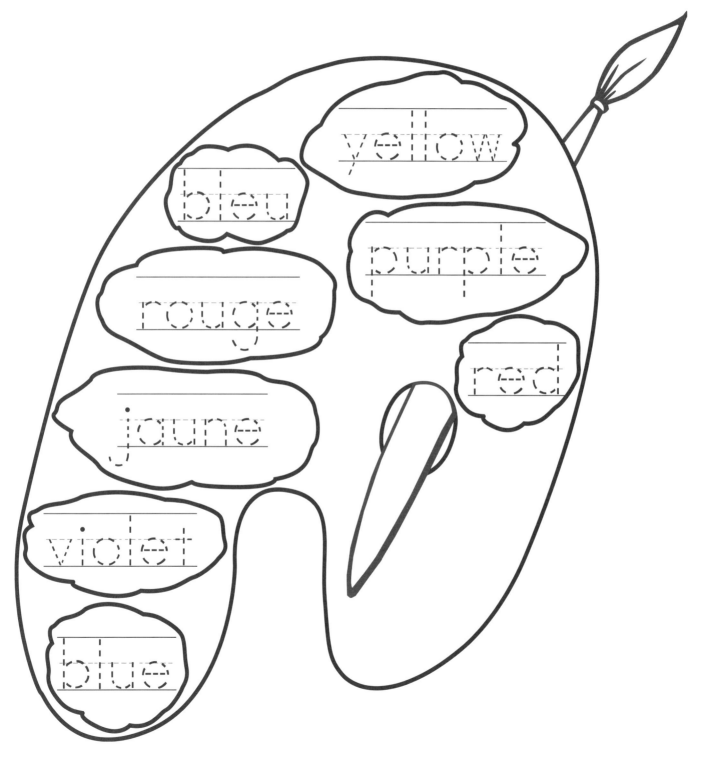

Bilingual Kids: English-French, Beginners   © 2010 Sara Jordan Publishing

Activity 2 / Activité 2

Color the balloons.

Colorie les ballons.

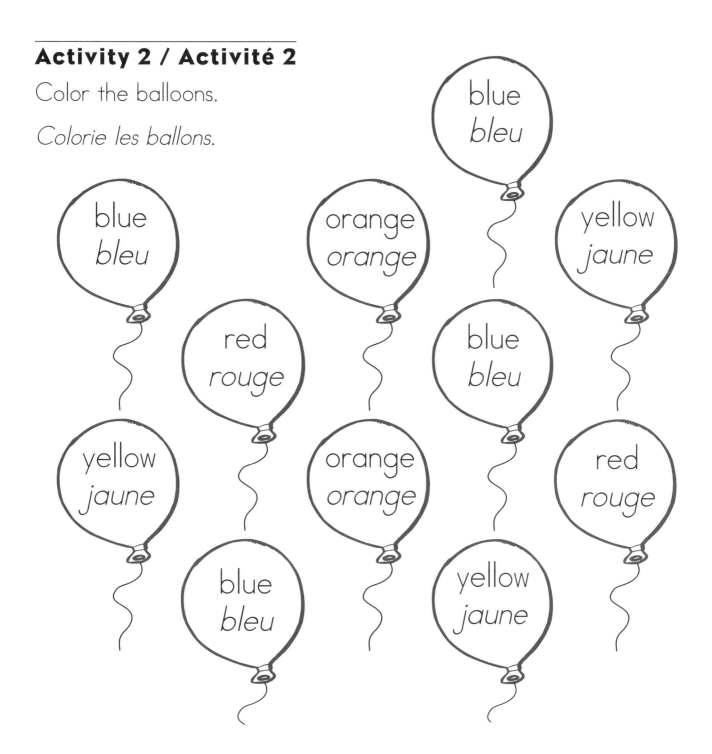

Combien y a-t-il de ballons rouges? _____

How many balloons are blue? _____

Combien y a-t-il de ballons jaunes? _____

How many balloons are orange? _____

Activity 3 / Activité 3

How many candles are on each birthday cake?

Combien y a-t-il de bougies sur chaque gâteau?

two   deux

   Bilingual Kids: English-French, Beginners   © 2010 Sara Jordan Publishing

Group Lesson

Materials: word cards (for the language being learned) using words from suggested vocabulary list, envelopes or sandwich bags, paper or plastic letters, white piece of paper, crayons

Preparation: Place a word card with its individual letters and blank piece of paper into each envelope or bag.

How it Works:
Review the vowels and their sounds. Hand out an envelope or bag to each student. Each student makes the word on the word card using the individual letters. Students print the word on the piece of paper and circle the vowels in each word. Students may continue by exchanging their bags with each other.

Activité de groupe

Matériel: Cartes avec les mots de la liste de vocabulaire (pour la langue qu'on apprend) des enveloppes ou des sacs en papier, des lettres en plastique ou en papier, une feuille de papier, des crayons de couleur

Préparation: Placez une carte avec un mot de la liste et ses lettres individuelles et une feuille de papier dans chaque enveloppe ou sac en papier.

Suggested Vocabulary List
Liste de vocabulaire

(l') abeille	bee
arrêter	to stop
(l') avion	airplane
(le) bateau	boat
(le) bébé	baby
(le) camion	truck
(la) cusinière	stove
(le) gâteau	cake
(le) lit	bed
(la) lumière	light
mon, ma, mes	my
(la) mule	mule
(la) nuit	night
pourquoi	why
(le) rateau	rake
répondre	to answer
rusé	sly
(la) toupie	top

Comment faire:
Révisez les voyelles et leurs sons. Distribuez une enveloppe ou un sac en papier à tous les élèves. Chaque élève fait le mot avec les lettres individuelles. Puis les élèves écrivent le mot sur la feuille de papier et encerclent les voyelles. Les élèves peuvent continuer à faire d'autres mots en énchangeant leur sac avec celui d'un autre élève.

Activity 1 / Activité 1

Print the numbers in your new language.
Circle any letter that is a vowel (a, e, i, o, u).

Écris les nombres dans ta langue.
Encercle toutes les voyelles (a, e, i, o, u).

1 one on _____ 7 _____

2 _____ 8 _____

3 _____ 9 _____

4 _____ 10 _____

5 _____ 11 _____

6 _____ 12 _____

Word Bank / Liste de mots

one / *un*	two / *deux*	three / *trois*	four / *quatre*	five / *cinq*	six / *six*
seven / *sept*	eight / *huit*	nine / *neuf*	ten / *dix*	eleven / *onze*	twelve / *douze*

Activity 2 / Activité 2

Print the words. Circle the long vowels in the English words. They say their names. Hint: vowels are a, e, i, o, u.

Écris les mots. Encercle les voyelles longues dans les mots anglais. Les voyelles sont a, e, i, o, u.

bee

(l') abeille

night

(la) nuit

plane

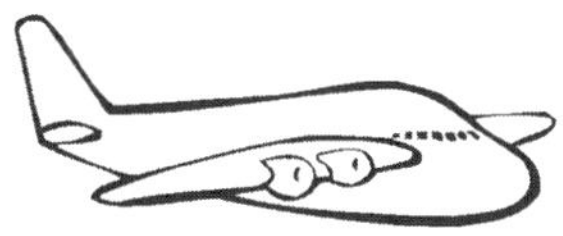

(l') avion

stove

(la) cuisinière

Activity 3 / Activité 3

These words sound the same. Print them and circle the rhyming parts.

Ces mots se ressemblent. Écris-les et encercle les rimes.

 top

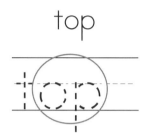

 stop

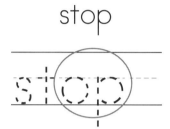

 light

night

(l') avion

(le) camion

(le) gâteau

(le) bateau

Word Bank / Liste de mots			
top / *la toupie*	stop / *stop*	light / *la lumière*	night / *la nuit*
plane / *l'avion*	truck / *le camion*	cake / *le gâteau*	boat / *le bateau*

Bilingual Kids: English-French, Beginners © 2010 Sara Jordan Publishing

Suggested Vocabulary List
Liste de vocabulaire

(le) cercle	circle
(les) cerises	cherries
(la) chaise	chair
(le) chat	cat
(le) chocolat	chocolate
(la) cité	city
(les) épices	spices
(le) fromage	cheese
(le) gâteau	cake
(la) police	police
(le) riz	rice
(les) souris	mice
(la) vache	cow

Group Lesson

Materials: individual letter cards for soft C /s/, hard C /k/ and CH for each student

Preparation: Each student requires three letter cards with each of the following C combinations: soft C /s/, hard C /k/ and CH.

How it Works:
Hand out three cards with each of the C combinations (soft C /s/, hard C /k/, CH) to each student. The teacher says a word in either French or English, i.e., "chemise" and the students hold up the correct card to show the sound in the word. Continue using the words from the suggested vocabulary list.

Activité de groupe

Matériel: des cartes avec C fort /k/, C doux /s/ et CH

Préparation: Chaque élève a besoin de trois cartes C fort /k/, C doux /s/ et CH.

Comment faire:
Donnez trois cartes avec C fort /k/, C doux /s/ et CH à chaque élève. Le professeur dit un mot en anglais ou en français, ex : « chemise » et les élèves montrent la carte avec le son du mot. Continuez en utilisant les mots de la liste.

Activity 1 / Activité 1

Print these words. Draw a square around the "hard C" (/k/ sound) and a circle around the "soft C" (/s/ sound) in the English words.

Écris les mots. Dessine un carré autour du C fort (le son k) et un cercle autour du C doux (le son ss) dans les mots anglais.

circle / *cercle*

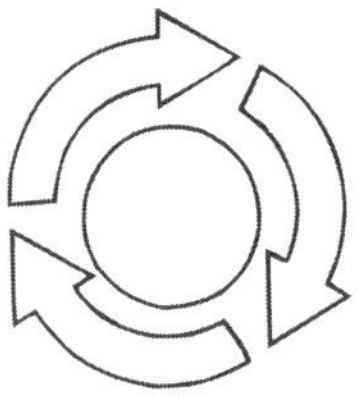

cow / *vache*

cat / *chat*

mice / *souris*

rice / *riz*

cake / *gâteau*

Word Bank / Liste de mots		
circle / *le cercle*	cow / *la vache*	cat / *le chat*
mice / *les souris*	rice / *le riz*	cake / *le gâteau*

Bilingual Kids: English–French, Beginners © 2010 Sara Jordan Publishing

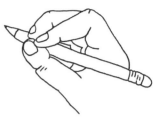

Activity 2 / Activité 2

Print and match these words.

Écris les mots et fais-les correspondre avec les images.

city

_____

- - - - - - - - - - - -

_____

(la) police

_____

- - - - - - - - - - - -

_____

spices

_____

- - - - - - - - - - - -

_____

(la) cité

_____

- - - - - - - - - - - -

_____

police

_____

- - - - - - - - - - - -

_____

(les) épices

_____

- - - - - - - - - - - -

_____

Word Bank / Liste de mots

| city / *la cité* | spices / *les épices* | police / *la police* |

Activity 3 / Activité 3

Print these words using red to trace CH in English and blue to trace CH in French.

Écris ces mots et trace CH en rouge en anglais et CH en bleu en français.

Word Bank / Liste de mots		
chocolate / *le chocolat*	shirt / *la chemise*	cherries / *les cerises*
chair / *la chaise*	cheese / *le fromage*	

Bilingual Kids: English–French, Beginners   © 2010 Sara Jordan Publishing

Suggested
Vocabulary List
Liste de vocabulaire

(les) bijoux	jewelry
(la) bougie	candle
(le) garçon	boy
(la) gare	train station
(le) gâteau	cake
(la) gazelle	gazelle
(le) géant	giant
(le) gel	gel
(la) gelée	jelly
(la) gemme	gem
(le) genou	knee
(le) gilet	sweater
(la) girafe	giraffe
(le) golf	golf
(la) gomme	eraser
(la) gorge	throat
(le) gorille	gorilla
(la) guêpe	wasp
(le/la) guide	guide
(la) guitare	guitar
(le) gus	guy
(le) jardin	garden
(le) jeu	game
(la) jupe	skirt
(le) jus	juice

Group Lesson

Materials: spinner, word cards with words from the suggested vocabulary list, pocket chart

Preparation: Print word cards from our website at: http://www.SongsThatTeach.com/BilingualFrenchWordCards
Make a spinner and divide it into six equal parts. Print the combinations: GA, GE, GI, GO, GU, J in each section.

How it Works:
Hand out French word cards to each student. Have one student spin the spinner and read the sound aloud. Ask the students for example, "Qui a un mot avec GA ?" Have students with French words containing GA read their words aloud and then display them on the board or in a pocket chart. When all the words have been displayed, sort the words into their different sounds.

Activité de groupe

Matériel: roue avec une flèche qui tourne au centre, cartes avec les mots de la liste

Préparation: Imprimez les cartes sur notre site web à : http://www.SongsThatTeach.com/BilingualFrenchWordCards
Faites une roue et divisez–la en six sections égales. Dans chaques section écrivez les lettres : GA, GE, GI, GO, GU, J.

Comment faire:
Distribuez les cartes en français aux élèves. Demandez à un élève de faire tourner la roue et de lire le son à haute voix. Demandez aux élèves : « Who has a word that contains GA? » Demandez aux élèves de lire leurs mots avec GA, puis de les mettre au tableau. Quand tous les mots sont au tableau, classez–les suivant les différents sons.

Activity 1 / Activité 1

Trace the words and match them up.

Écris les mots et fais–les correspondre.

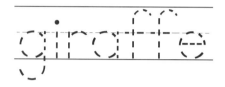

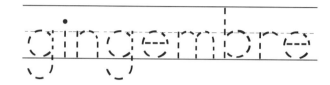

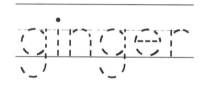

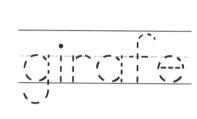 

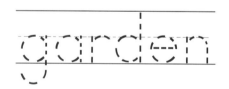

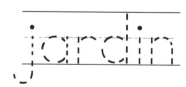 

Word Bank / Liste de mots

giraffe / *la girafe*   ginger / *le gingembre*   garden / *le jardin*   game / *le jeu*

Bilingual Kids: English–French, Beginners   © 2010 Sara Jordan Publishing

Activity 2 / Activité 2

Print and say aloud these words with G followed by A, O or U.

Écris et dis à haute voix ces mots avec G suivi par A, O ou U.

guy

le gamin

gorilla

le gorille

Print and say aloud these words with G followed by I or E.

Écris et dis à haute voix ces mots avec G suivi par I ou E.

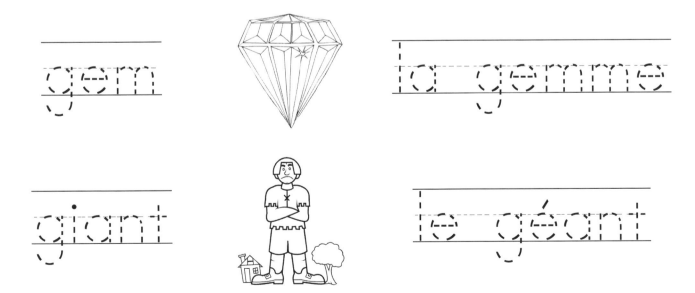

gem

la gemme

giant

le géant

Activity 3 / Activité 3

Complete the sentences using hints from the word bank below.

Complète les phrases avec les mots de la liste.

Julie drinks juice,

Julie boit du jus,

wears _____ ,

porte _____ ,

and eats _____ .

et mange _____ .

Word Bank / Liste de mots	
jewelry / *des bijoux*	jelly / *de la gelée*

Bilingual Kids: English-French, Beginners   © 2010 Sara Jordan Publishing

Group Lesson

Materials: large clock, small clock for each student (optional)

How it Works:

Show a time on the clock and say, "Quelle heure est-il?" followed by, "What time is it?" so that the children know the question in both languages. Begin showing time to the hour only. Example: Display the time 5:00 on the clock and say, "It is 5:00 o'clock," followed by "Il est cinq heures." Continue in this way until they can confidently state the time to the hour in both languages and then follow with the half and quarter hour. A variation is to give all of the students a clock and have them show a time that is given to them in both languages.

Activité de groupe

Matériel: une grande horloge, une petite horloge pour chaque élève (facultatif)

Comment faire:

Montrez l'heure sur l'horloge et dites : « What time is it? », suivi de, « Quelle heure est-il? » pour que les élèves apprennent la question dans les deux langues. Commencez par montrer les heures. Exemple : montrez 5h00 sur l'horloge et dites : « Il est cinq heures », suivi de, « It is 5 o'clock ». Continuez jusqu'à ce qu'ils sachent bien dire les heures puis ajoutez : et quart, et demie et moins le quart. Vous pouvez aussi donner une horloge à chaque élève et chaque élèves peut indiquer l'heure que vous lui donnez dans les deux langues.

Suggested Vocabulary List
Liste de vocabulaire

(l') aquarium	aquarium
(le) carré	square
(l') écureuil	squirrel
(l') édredon	quilt
(le) fromage	cheese
(le) paquet	parcel
(le) parc	park
(la) plume	quill
(la) quille	bowling pin
quinze	fifteen
(la) raquette	racket
(la) reine	queen
(l') horloge	clock
et demie	half past
et quart	quarter past
moins le quart	quarter to

Activity 1 / Activité 1

Did you know that the QU combination in French sounds like /k/ in English?

Savais–tu que les lettres QU en français se prononcent comme le /k/ en anglais ?

Say these words aloud and print them.

Dis ces mots à haute voix et écris–les.

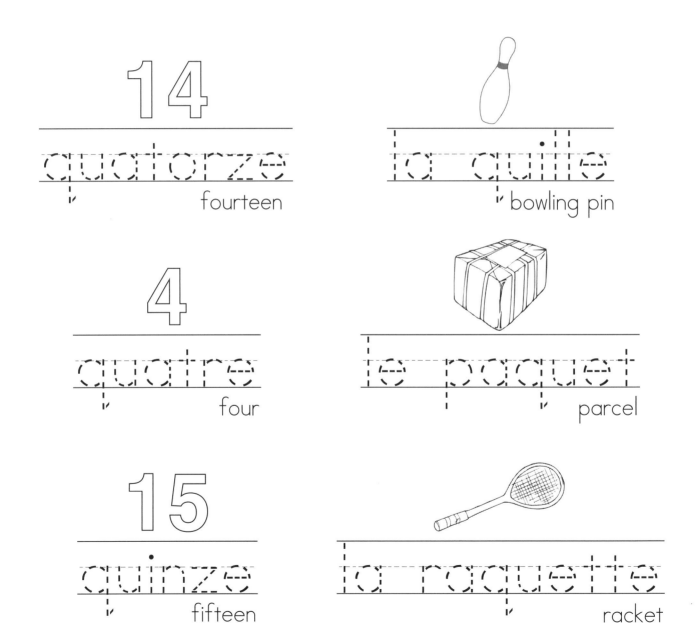

14
quatorze
fourteen

la quille
bowling pin

4
quatre
four

le paquet
parcel

15
quinze
fifteen

la raquette
racket

Bilingual Kids: English-French, Beginners   © 2010 Sara Jordan Publishing

Activity 2 / Activité 2

> The QU combination in English sounds like /kw/.
>
> *Les lettres QU en anglais se prononcent /kw/.*

Say these words aloud and print them.

Dis ces mots à haute voix et écris–les.

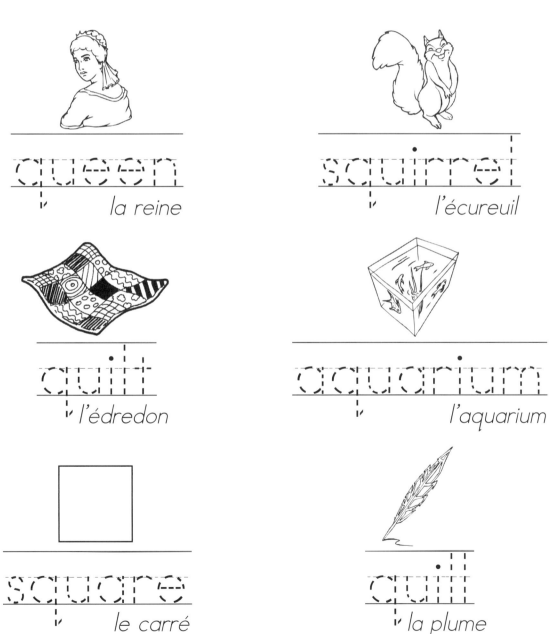

queen
la reine

squirrel
l'écureuil

quilt
l'édredon

aquarium
l'aquarium

square
le carré

quill
la plume

Activity 3 / Activité 3

Print the words and draw the time on the clocks.

Écris les mots et indique l'heure dans les horloges

 *Il est*

cinq heures.

 *Il est*

six heures et quart.

 *Il est*

sept heures et demie.

Word Bank / Liste de mots	
five o'clock / *cinq heures*	quarter past six / *six heures et quart*
half past seven / *sept heures et demie*	clock / *l'horloge*

Bilingual Kids: English-French, Beginners   © 2010 Sara Jordan Publishing

Suggested Vocabulary List
Liste de vocabulaire

(la) bêche	spade
(le) café	coffee
(la) chèvre	goat
(la) crêpe	crepe
(le) bébé	baby
(l') école	school
(l') écureuil	squirrel
(la) flèche	arrow
(le) gâteau	cake
(la) pêche	peach
(la) règle	ruler
(la) télévision	television
(la) tête	head
(le) zèbre	zebra

Group Lesson

Materials: word cards using words with accents from suggested vocabulary list

Preparation: Print word cards from our website at: http://www.SongsThatTeach.com/BilingualFrenchWordCards

How it Works:
This activity is played like the game Simon Says. First go over the actions of the three different accents: *aigu*, *grave* and *circonflexe* with the students. Begin by saying, "Simon says show me an accent aigu" and the students place their arms in that position. Once they are confident with the accent hand positions, hold up word cards with words containing accents, like the word école, and say, "Simon says show me the accent in the word école." Once all students are in the correct position, have them call out the name of the accent. To make the game more challenging, have students sit down when they display the wrong hand position or accent name and play until there is only one student left standing.

Activité de groupe

Matériel: cartes avec les mots avec accents de la liste de vocabulaire

Préparation: Imprimez les cartes sur notre site web à : http://www.SongsThatTeach.com/BilingualFrenchWordCards

Comment faire:
Cette activité se joue comme « Simon dit ». Revoyez les actions pour les trois accents, *aigu*, *grave* et *circonflexe* avec les élèves. Vous dites : « Simon dit: montrez-moi un accent aigu » et les élèves placent leurs mains dans la bonne position. Quand ils connaissent bien la position des mains pour chaque accent, montrez les cartes avec les mots qui ont des accents, comme le mot « école » et dites: « Simon dit: montrez-moi l'accent dans l'école ». Quand tous les élèves sont dans la bonne position demandez-leur de dire le nom de l'accent. Pour rendre le jeu plus difficile, faites asseoir les élèves qui se sont trompés et jouez jusqu'à ce qu'il reste un(e) seul élève debout.

Activity 1 / Activité 1

Draw lines to match the accents to their names.

Avec une ligne joins l'accent et son nom.

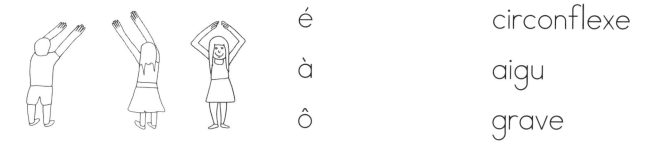

é   circonflexe

à   aigu

ô   grave

Trace each word and draw the correct accents in the circles.

Trace chaque mot et écris la bonne forme de l'accent dans les cercles.

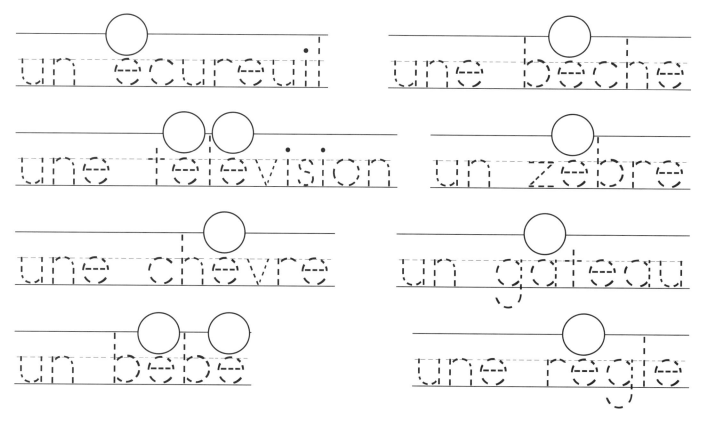

un écureuil   une bêche

une télévision   un zèbre

une chèvre   un gâteau

un bébé   une règle

Bilingual Kids: English–French, Beginners   © 2010 Sara Jordan Publishing

Activity 2 / Activité 2

Fill in the missing letters with the correct accents.

Complète avec les lettres manquantes avec les bons accents.

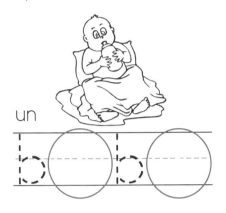

un

un

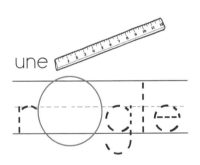

une

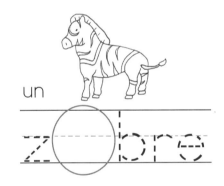

un

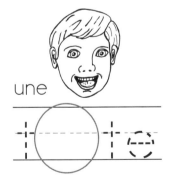

une

une

Word Bank / *Liste de mots*		
baby / *un bébé*	squirrel / *un écureuil*	ruler / *une règle*
zebra / *un zèbre*	head / *une tête*	peach / *une pêche*

Activity 3 / Activité 3

Trace each word using blue for words with accent aigu, red for words with accent grave and yellow for words with accent circonflexe.

Trace chaque mot en bleu pour les mots avec un accent aigu, en rouge pour les mots avec un accent grave et en jaune pour les mots avec un accent circonflexe.

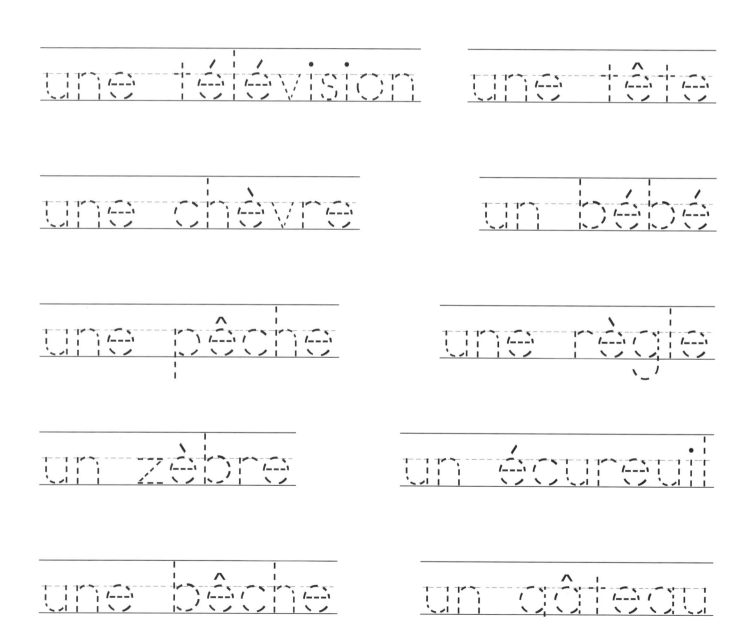

Bilingual Kids: English-French, Beginners © 2010 Sara Jordan Publishing

Suggested Vocabulary List
Liste de vocabulaire

(un) âne	donkey
(une) baleine	whale
(un) canard	duck
(un) castor	beaver
(un) chat	cat
(un) cheval	horse
(une) chèvre	goat
(un) chien	dog
(un) coyote	coyote
(un) dauphin	dolphin
(une) dinde	turkey
(un) élan	moose
(une) grenouille	frog
(un) lapin	rabbit
(un) loup	wolf
(un) lynx	lynx
(une) moufette	skunk
(un) mouton	sheep
(un) oiseau	bird
(un) ours	bear
(un) papillon	butterfly
(un) poisson	fish
(un) poulet	chicken
(un) raton laveur	raccoon
(un) renard	fox
(un) serpent	snake
(une) vache	cow

Group Lesson

Materials: picture cards and word cards of the various animals in the suggested vocabulary list, pocket chart

Preparation: Display the animal word cards in the pocket chart.

How it Works:
Go over the names of the animals in both languages as a review. A student chooses an animal picture card and imitates or makes the sound of that animal. Students need to guess the name of the animal in French. Once a student has guessed the animal, place the picture card in the pocket chart and have a student match the word card to the picture card. For extra movement, have all students become the animal.

Activité de groupe

Matériel: cartes avec des images d'animaux et cartes avec les noms des animaux de la liste de vocabulaire, tableau en carton avec des pochettes

Préparation: Placez les cartes avec les noms des animaux dans les pochettes du tableau.

Comment faire:
Faites apprendre les noms des animaux aux élèves dans les deux langues. Un étudiant choisit un animal et imite cet animal ou pousse son cri. Les élèves doivent deviner le nom de l'animal en français. Quand un élève a bien deviné l'animal, placez la carte de l'animal dans une pochette du tableau et faites-lui trouver la carte avec le nom de l'animal. Vous pouvez demander aux élèves d'imiter l'animal pour un peu d'animation.

Activity 1 / Activité 1

Talk a walk along the path. Use the word bank to help you list what you see in your new language.

Promène-toi et écris dans ta nouvelle langue ce que tu vois à l'aide de la liste de mots.

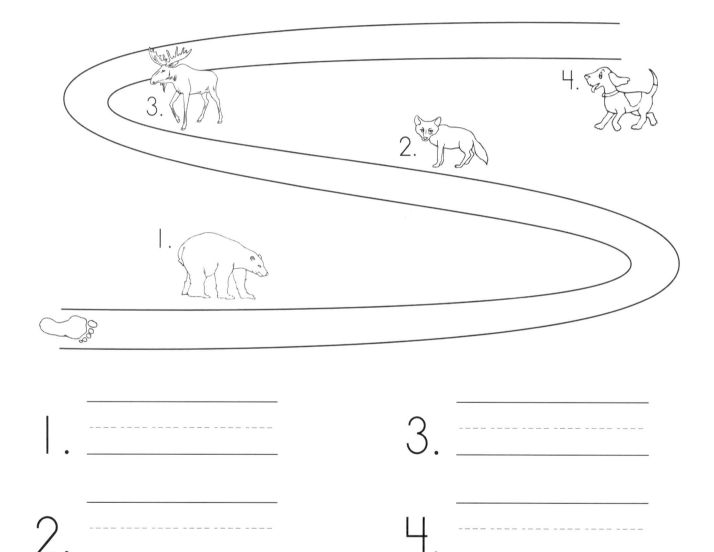

1. _____

2. _____

3. _____

4. _____

Word Bank / Liste de mots			
fox / *un renard*	moose / *un élan*	dog / *un chien*	bear / *un ours*

Bilingual Kids: English-French, Beginners © 2010 Sara Jordan Publishing

Activity 2 / Activité 2

Complete the crossword puzzle.

Complète les mots croisés.

ACROSS / HORIZONTALES

2. une chèvre (English)
5. un élan (English)
7. rabbit (French)
8. coyote (French)

DOWN / VERTICALES

1. un chien (English)
3. bear (French)
4. chicken (French)
6. un renard (English)

Word Bank / Liste de mots			
bear / un ours	moose / un élan	coyote / un coyote	chicken / un poulet
dog / un chien	rabbit / un lapin	fox / un renard	goat / une chèvre

Activity 3 / Activité 3

Fill in the blanks in French to find the name of a pointy animal.

Écris les noms des animaux en français et tu trouveras le nom d'un animal qui pique.

porcupine

Word Bank / Liste de mots			porcupine / *un porc–épic*
bear / un ours	moose / un élan	horse / un cheval	chicken / un poulet
dog / un chien	rabbit / un lapin	fox / un renard	goat / une chèvre

Bilingual Kids: English-French, Beginners © 2010 Sara Jordan Publishing

Group Lesson

Materials: bag or container, word cards with words from the suggested vocabulary list

Preparation: Print word cards from our website at: http://www.SongsThatTeach.com/ BilingualFrenchWordCards Place the word cards in the bag.

How it Works:

Students sit in a circle. Hand the bag to a student and have them pull a card out of the bag. The student reads the word aloud to the group and asks a student the opposite. If the answer is correct, he/she gets the bad, chooses a new word and the game continues until all the words have been taken out of the bag. This activity can be done in either French or English.

Activité de groupe

Matériel: sac ou boîte, cartes avec les mots de la liste de vocabulaire

Préparation: Imprimez les cartes sur notre site web à : http://www.SongsThatTeach.com/ BilingualFrenchWordCards

Comment faire:

Les élèves sont assis en cercle. Donnez le sac à un(e) élève pour qu'il/elle sorte une carte. L'élève lit le mot à haute voix et demande à un(e) élève le contraire. Si la réponse est correcte, on lui donne le sac, il choisit un autre mot et le jeu continue. Le jeu finit quand il n'y a plus aucun mot dans le sac. On peut faire cette activité en français ou en anglais.

Suggested Vocabulary List
Liste de vocabulaire

bas	low
beau	beautiful
bon	good
court	short
étroit	narrow
gentil	nice
grand	tall
gros	big
haut	high
heureux	happy
laid	ugly
large	wide
léger	light
lent	slow
lourd	heavy
mauvais	bad
méchant	naughty
petit	small
rapide	fast
salé	salty
sucré	sweet
triste	sad

Activity 1 / Activité 1

Print the French opposites into the shape puzzles.

Écris les contraires en français dans les cases.

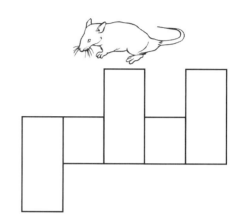

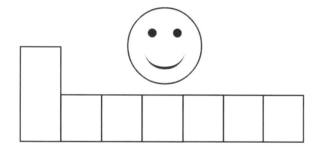

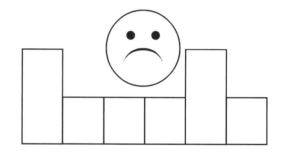

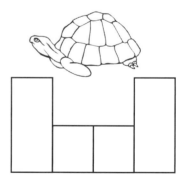

Word Bank / Liste de mots		
happy / heureux	fast / rapide	big / grand
small / petit	sad / triste	slow / lent

Bilingual Kids: English-French, Beginners   © 2010 Sara Jordan Publishing

Activity 2 / Activité 2

Draw lines to match the opposites.

Tire des lignes pour faire correspondre les contraires.

 léger

bas

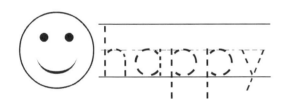 happy

tall

 short

lourd

 haut

sad

Activity 3 / Activité 3

Answer the questions below. Your hints are in the word bank.

Réponds aux questions suivants. Les indices sont dans la liste.

1. *Quel est le contraire de lourd ?* _____

2. What is the opposite of high? _____

3. *Quel est le contraire de gros ?* _____

4. What is the opposite of slow? _____

5. *Quel est le contraire de court ?* _____

6. What is the opposite of happy? _____

7. *Quel est le contraire de triste ?* _____

8. What is the opposite of tall? _____

9. *Quel est le contraire de grand ?* _____

Word Bank / Liste de mots

fast / rapide	light / léger	low / bas	small / petit
short / court	happy / heureux	sad / triste	grand / tall

Bilingual Kids: English–French, Beginners   © 2010 Sara Jordan Publishing

Group Lesson

Materials: a set of food and family word cards with pictures (a set each in French and English) from the suggested vocabulary list, a bag

Preparation: Print word cards from our website at: http://www.SongsThatTeach.com/BilingualFrenchWordCards

How it Works:
Put words into a bag and have each student choose a card. Students look for their partners with the same word in the other language. Students practice saying their word in both languages and then share their words with the group.

Activité de groupe

Matériel: un ensemble de cartes avec des mots et des images de nourriture et de famille (un ensemble en français et un ensemble en anglais), un sac

Préparation: Imprimez les cartes sur notre site web à: http://www.SongsThatTeach.com/BilingualFrenchWordCards

Comment faire:
Mettez les cartes avec les mots dans un sac. Chaque élève choisit une carte. Les élèves cherchent leur partenaire avec le même mot mais dans l'autre langue. Les élèves apprennent et répètent leur mot dans les deux langues et partagent leur mot avec le groupe.

Suggested Vocabulary List
Liste de vocabulaire

(la) banane	banana
(le) brocoli	broccoli
(le) cousin	cousin
(le) dîner	dinner
(les) fèves	beans
(le) fils	son
(la) grand-mère	grandmother
(le) grand-père	grandfather
jaune	yellow
(le) lait	milk
(la) laitue	lettuce
(le) maïs	corn
(la) mère	mother
(les) oeufs	eggs
(l') oncle	uncle
(le) pain	bread
(le) père	father
(le) petit déjeuner	breakfast
(le) poisson	fish
(la) pomme	appe
(le) riz	rice
rouge	red
(la) salade	salad
(le) sel	salt
(la) soeur	sister
(la) soupe	soup
(le) sucre	sugar
(la) tante	aunt
vert	green

Activity 1 / Activité 1

Complete the family tree with the words in the word bank.

Complète l'arbre généalogique avec les mots de la liste.

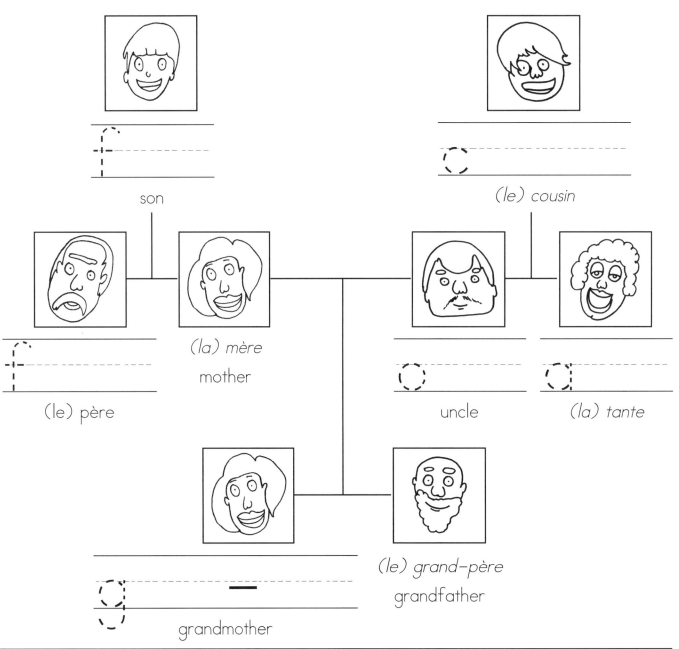

son

(le) cousin

(le) père

(la) mère
mother

uncle

(la) tante

grandmother

(le) grand-père
grandfather

Word Bank / Liste de mots		
son / *le fils*	father / *le père*	grandmother / *la grand-mère*
aunt / *la tante*	uncle / *l'oncle*	cousin / *le cousin*

Bilingual Kids: English-French, Beginners © 2010 Sara Jordan Publishing

Activity 2 / Activité 2

Complete the crossword puzzle.

Complète les mots croisés.

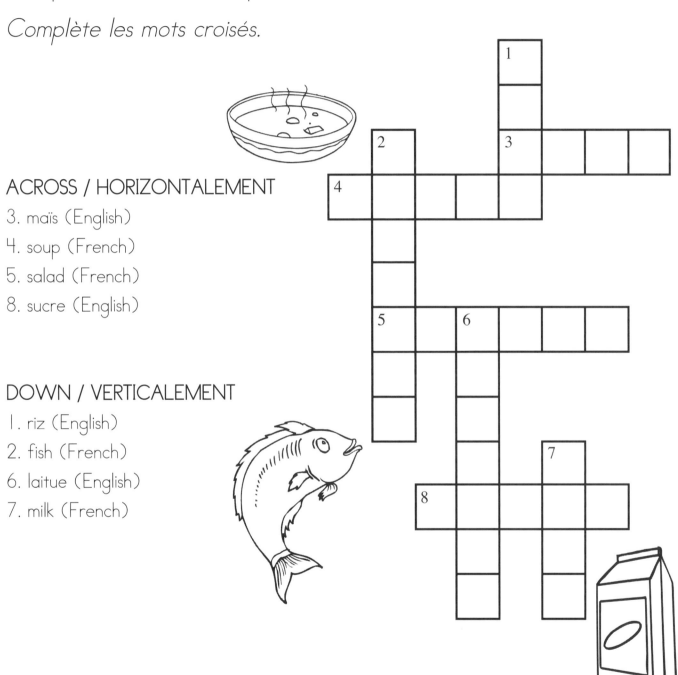

ACROSS / HORIZONTALEMENT

3. maïs (English)

4. soup (French)

5. salad (French)

8. sucre (English)

DOWN / VERTICALEMENT

1. riz (English)

2. fish (French)

6. laitue (English)

7. milk (French)

Word Bank / Liste de mots

| soup / *la soupe* | fish / *le poisson* | salad / *la salade* | corn / *le maïs* |
| rice / *le riz* | sugar / *le sucre* | milk / *le lait* | lettuce / *la laitue* |

Activity 3 / Activité 3

Color the object that does not belong. Then print this word to the side. Use your new language.

Colorie ce qui est différent, puis trouve le mot dans la liste et écris-le à côté dans ta nouvelle langue.

eggs /
(les) oeufs

brother /
(le) frère

beans /
(les) fèves

sister /
(la) soeur

mother /
(la) mère

bread /
(le) pain

apple /
(la) pomme

banana /
(la) banane

salt /
(le) sel

grandfather /
(le) grand-père

dinner /
(le) dîner

breakfast /
(le) petit déjeuner

Bilingual Kids: English-French, Beginners   © 2010 Sara Jordan Publishing

CHAPTER 11

Activity 4 / Activité 4

Fill in the missing vowels. Color the pictures.

Écris les mots en ajoutant les voyelles. Colorie les images.

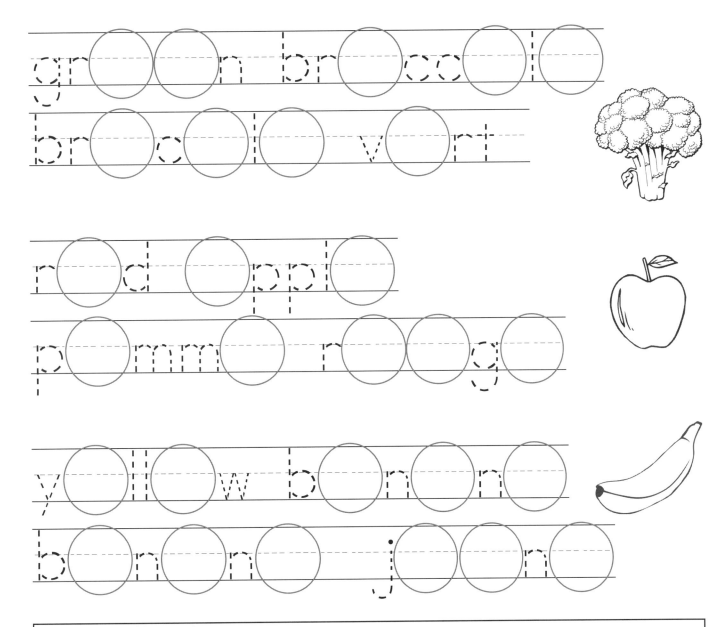

Word Bank / Liste de mots

banana / *la banane*	broccoli / *le brocoli*	apple / *la pomme*
green / *vert*	red / *rouge*	yellow / *jaune*

Activity 5 / Activité 5

Find all the words in the word search.

Trouve tous les mots.

```
P  F  R  È  R  E  G  R  P  M  S  G  S  C
S  I  J  G  F  I  L  L  E  O  O  R  I  S
F  L  X  R  T  H  A  U  N  T  N  A  S  D
Q  S  A  A  B  W  D  P  Q  H  C  N  T  A
G  R  A  N  D  -  M  È  R  E  L  D  E  U
F  C  Z  D  V  E  K  R  D  R  E  F  R  G
A  O  I  -  M  È  R  E  F  N  H  A  R  H
T  U  P  P  S  O  N  L  T  A  N  T  E  T
H  S  M  È  B  R  O  T  H  E  R  H  I  E
E  I  G  R  A  N  D  M  O  T  H  E  R  R
R  N  W  E  U  N  C  L  E  L  M  R  S  W
S  O  E  U  R  O  U  I  C  O  U  S  I  N
```

father	père	grandmother	grand-mère	aunt	tante
mother	mère	grandfather	grand-père	uncle	oncle
sister	soeur	son	fils	cousin	cousin
brother	frère	daughter	fille		

Bilingual Kids: English-French, Beginners   © 2010 Sara Jordan Publishing

Group Lesson

How it Works:
Have your students stand in a group facing you. Alternate giving directions in English and Spanish. For example, start by saying, "Simon dit, touchez votre nez" or "Simon says, touch your nose." Continue until the students confidently know their body parts in both languages.

Activité de groupe

Comment faire:
Les élèves sont debout en face de vous. Donnez alternativement les instructions en anglais et en français. Par exemple, vous dites : « Simon says, touch your nose » ou « Simon dit, touchez votre nez ». Continuez jusqu'à ce que les élèves sachent très bien les parties du corps dans les deux langues.

Suggested Vocabulary List
Liste de vocabulaire

(la) bouche	mouth
(les) bras	arms
(les) épaules	shoulders
(les) jambes	legs
(les) mains	hands
(le) nez	nose
(les) pieds	feet
(les) oreilles	ears
(les) orteils	toes
(la) tête	head
(les) yeux	eyes

Activity 1 / Activité 1

Name the parts of the body. Use the words in the word bank.

Nomme les parties du corps. Utilise les mots dans la liste de vocabulaire.

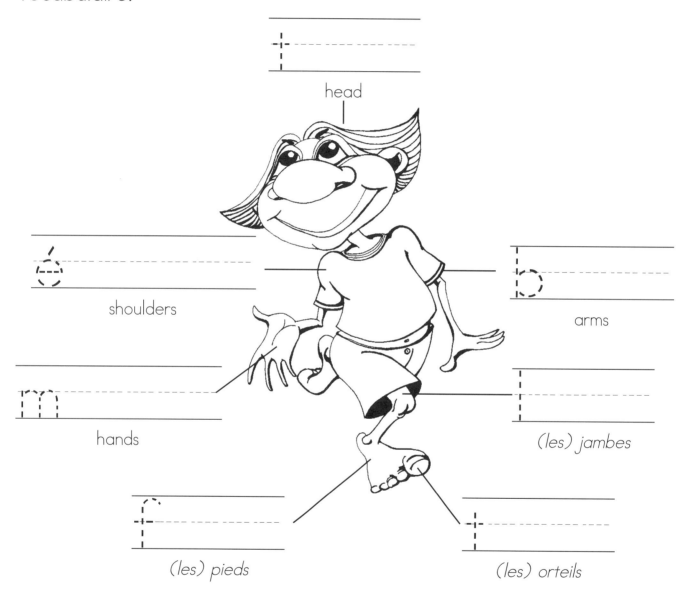

head

shoulders

arms

hands

(les) jambes

(les) pieds

(les) orteils

Word Bank / Liste de mots

head / *la tête*	legs / *les jambes*	shoulders / *les épaules*
feet / *les pieds*	arms / *les bras*	toes / *les orteils*
hands / *les mains*		

Bilingual Kids: English-French, Beginners © 2010 Sara Jordan Publishing

Activity 2 / Activité 2

Match the words with the pictures. Then print the word in your new language.

Fais correspondre les mots avec les images. Écris ensuite le mot dans ta nouvelle langue.

les yeux
eyes

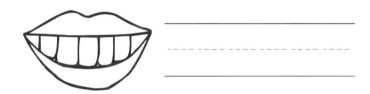

les oreilles
ears

la bouche
mouth

le nez
nose

Activity 3 / Activité 3

Print the French words into the shape puzzles.

Écris les mots en français dans les cases.

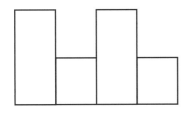
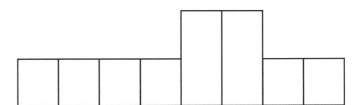

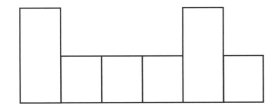
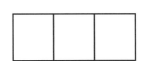

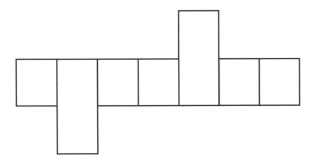
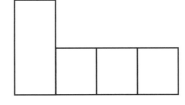

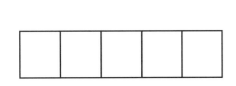
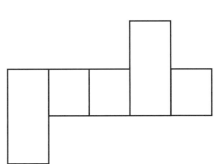

Word Bank / Liste de mots		
shoulders / *les épaules*	feet / *les pieds*	head / *la tête*
arms / *les bras*	nose / *le nez*	hands / *les mains*
ears / *les oreilles*	mouth / *la bouche*	

   Bilingual Kids: English–French, Beginners © 2010 Sara Jordan Publishing

Answer Keys / Réponses

Pg. 13
bonne nuit
de rien
merci
ça va bien
au revoir

Pg. 14

How are you? / Comment ça va ?	I'm well. / Ça va bien
See you later! / À plus tard !	Good-bye. / Au revoir.

Pg. 19

English	Français
eight	cinq
eleven	deux
five	dix
four	douze
nine	huit
one	neuf
seven	onze
six	quatre
ten	sept
three	six
twelve	trois
two	un

Pg. 20
boy / le garçon
horse / le cheval
jacket / la veste
egg / l'oeuf

Pg. 24

two	deux
four	quatre
seven	sept
three	trois
ten	dix
five	cinq

Pg. 36
Julie drinks juice,
Julie boit du jus,
wears jewelry
porte des bijoux
and eats jelly.
et mange de la gelée.

Pg. 42

un écureuil	une bêche
une télévision	un zèbre
une chèvre	un gâteau
un bébé	une règle

Pg. 43

un bébé	un écureuil
une règle	un zèbre
une tête	une pêche

Pg. 46
1. bear / un ours
2. fox / un renard
3. moose / un élan
4. dog / un chien

Pg. 47
Across
2. goat
5. moose
7. lapin
8. coyote
Down
1. dog
3. ours
4. poulet
6. fox

Pg. 48
poulet
ours
renard
chevel
–
élan
lapin
chien
chevre

Pg. 50

gros	petit
heureux	triste
rapide	lent

Pg. 52
1. léger
2. low
3. petit
4. fast
5. grand
6. sad
7. heureux
8. short
9. court

Pg. 55
Across
3. corn
4. soupe
5. salade
8. sugar
Down
1. rice
2. poisson
6. lettuce
7. lait

Pg. 56
brother / le frère
bread / le pain
salt / le sel
grandfather / le grand-père

Pg. 58

Pg. 62

tête	oreilles
bouche	nez
épaules	bras
mains	pieds

Ask your retailer about other excellent titles by Sara Jordan!

Bilingual Songs: English–French Series

This collection of songs, sung in both English and French, will have your students speaking, singing and laughing in French! Each CD & lyrics book kit covers different subjects ranging from the alphabet, counting, colors, opposites, shapes and sizes to gender, articles, adverbs and question words. CDs include accompaniment tracks perfect for class performances. Companion reproducible resource/ activity books are available, further enhancing what is learned in each of the songs.

Français pour débutants

Great for beginners! Learn the alphabet, farm animals, counting, family members, parts of the body, days of the week, colors, fruit, opposites and shapes in French. Perfect for students of all ages who want to learn a new language. The companion reproducible resource/activity book, French for Kids: Beginning Lessons, further reinforces what is learned in each of the songs.

Chansons thématiques pour apprendre la langue

This album of phenomenal singing teaches common expressions, clothing, meals, modes of transportation, weather, parts of the body, pets and rooms in the house. There is even a song teaching the correct use of prepositions! This is an interesting and useful album for beginning French speakers of any age. The companion reproducible resource/activity book, French for Kids: Thematic Lessons, further reinforces what is learned in each of the songs.

Visit us online to shop, listen and learn.

Our websites, www.SongsThatTeach.com and www.AprendeCantando.com, offer:
- an opportunity to purchase our resources online
- a biweekly newsletter including free songs
  downloads and activities
- free worksheets based on our educational songs
  which may be printed and shared with your class
- cartooning lessons, pen pal exchanges and contests
- healthy snack ideas
- information regarding educational standards
- links to other valuable websites

For further information or to request a free catalog, please call us toll-free at 1-800-567-7733 or write to:

Sara Jordan Publishing
M.P.O. Box 490
Niagara Falls, NY
U.S.A. 14302-0490

Sara Jordan Publishing
Station M, Box 160
Toronto, ON
Canada M6S 4T3